Mit Wörterbuch und Vokabelhilfe

Elisabeth Zöller

Englisch lernen mit den *Leselöwen* Tierfreundegeschichten

Aus dem Deutschen übersetzt von David Ingram
Zeichnungen von Wilfried Gebhard

Bibliografische Information Der Deutschen Bibliothek
Die Deutsche Bibliothek verzeichnet diese Publikation in der
Deutschen Nationalbibliografie; detaillierte bibliografische Daten
sind im Internet über *http://dnb.ddb.de* abrufbar.

*Der Umwelt zuliebe ist dieses Buch
auf chlorfrei gebleichtem Papier gedruckt.*

ISBN 3-7855-5331-5 – 1. Auflage 2005
© 2005 Loewe Verlag GmbH, Bindlach
Die deutsche Originalausgabe erschien 2001 im Loewe Verlag
unter dem Titel „Leselöwen-Tierfreundegeschichten"
Aus dem Deutschen übersetzt von David Ingram
Umschlagillustration: Wilfried Gebhard
Umschlaggestaltung: Andreas Henze

www.loewe-verlag.de

Contents

Mummy, what are pets? 11
Snow White has a baby 15
The chocolate bunny hunt 23
The walk 28
Oscar the kitten 35
The dog in the church 42
Felix is back 46
The snake in the loo 56

Liebe Eltern,

unaufhaltsam hält die englische Sprache Einzug in den kindlichen Wortschatz. Was die Sprachwissenschaft nüchtern als Anglizismen betitelt, finden die Kinder überaus spannend. Mit ungebremstem Wissensdurst machen sie sich daran, erste Worte oder Sätze in einer Fremdsprache zu erlernen und zu kommunizieren.

Kinder sind relativ früh mit dem Englischen vertraut, spätestens seit der Einführung des Englischunterrichts an den Grundschulen. Eine Fremdsprache spielerisch, ohne Erfolgszwang, dafür aber mit schnellen Erfolgserlebnissen lernen, so lautet das Motto.
Dieses Prinzip haben wir auch den Englisch-Ausgaben unserer Erstlese-Reihe *Leselöwen* zu Grunde gelegt. In abgeschlossenen Geschichten können die kindlichen Leser ihre ersten Englischkenntnisse anwenden und vertiefen. Die Sprache ist einfach gehalten, die wichtigsten Vokabeln sind im Text markiert und werden in ihrer konkreten Bedeutung am Rand auf Deutsch erklärt. Verben werden dabei gleich in der jeweiligen Person, Adjektive in der flektierten

Form übersetzt. Der Sinn eines Satzes lässt sich so schnell und ohne lästiges Nachschlagen erschließen. Viele Begriffe werden zusätzlich in den Illustrationen durch Wort-Bildzuweisungen erläutert.

Im Anhang finden sich sowohl die wichtigsten Vokabeln aus dem Text in alphabetischer Reihenfolge als auch ein speziell dem jeweiligen Thema zu Grunde gelegter Wortschatz auf einer praktischen Ausklappseite.

Die Verben stehen hier im Infinitiv, da an dieser Stelle der Hauptakzent eher auf der Erweiterung des Wortschatzes als auf der Erschließung eines Wortes innerhalb eines Satzes liegt. Dabei werden nicht alle möglichen Bedeutungen im Deutschen angegeben, sondern nur die wichtigsten.

Und wenn Sie mit Ihrem Kind gleichzeitig auch das Hörverständnis und die Sprechfertigkeit trainieren möchten, sind bei Jumbo zu jedem englischen *Leselöwen*-Band die entsprechenden Hörkassetten erhältlich.

Viel Spaß und Erfolg mit
„Englisch lernen mit den Leselöwen"
wünscht Ihnen Ihr

Leselöwen-Englisch-Team

Mummy, what are pets?

"Mummy, what are pets?"
   Mummy is tired today.   *müde*
The telephone rings all the time and she always answers it.
   "Mummy, what are pets?"
   And because Mummy is so tired, she says: "Pets are animals that live in the house."
   The next day Sarah hears a buzzing noise. A very loud   *surrendes Geräusch*
buzzing noise. Sarah
is frightened. She waves   *hat Angst; schwenkt*
her hand. Then a wasp stings   *Wespe; sticht*
Sarah. On her hand.

"Ow!" she shouts. It really hurts. Her hand starts to swell. Mummy cools it with cold water. Then she looks in the cupboard for a cream. She puts it on Sarah's hand.

Sarah tries to move her hand. It hurts. It is very swollen.

Sarah thinks for a while. Then she remembers something important.

tut weh
anzuschwellen;
kühlt

angeschwollen

eine Zeit lang

erinnert sich an

Wichtiges

"Mummy," she asks, "is a wasp a pet?"

Her mother laughs, and hugs Sarah. "No, a wasp is not a pet."

"But it lives in the house."

"Well, yes," her mother says. "But a wasp cannot live with people. It cannot get used to them."

"I see. You can't cuddle a wasp," Sarah says. "But you can cuddle a rabbit or a hamster."

"That's right," her mother says. "But you can't cuddle a budgie."

umarmt

gewöhnt sich nicht

schmusen

Wellensittich

"No, but you can talk to it," Sarah says. "And it twitters, and flies, and makes a lot of noise. A bit like a friend."

"That's right," her mother says.

Sarah has a long think. Then she says: "Mummy, I want a pet for my birthday."

"All right, Sarah, then you can have one," her mother says.

Sarah wants a pet to talk with, to play with, and to cuddle all day long!

zwitschert

Lärm

schmusen

Snow White has a baby

Uta has a big white rabbit called Snow White. It lives in comfortable straw, inside a special rabbit hutch.

The rabbit is soft and cuddly, and always eats its food. But Uta thinks it is lonely. One day, she decides to put another rabbit in the hutch.

A child at Uta's school says: "It is dangerous to put two rabbits together. Sometimes rabbits fight each other."

mit Namen Schneewittchen	
bequemen Stroh	
Kaninchenstall	
kuschelig	
beschließt	

15

But Uta decides to put a rabbit called Bommel into Snow White's hutch.

Bommel is a rabbit with reddish-brown fur. He is smaller than Snow White.

The two rabbits do not fight. They like each other.

beschließt	
mit Namen	
Schneewittchens	
rotbraunem Fell	
streiten sich nicht	

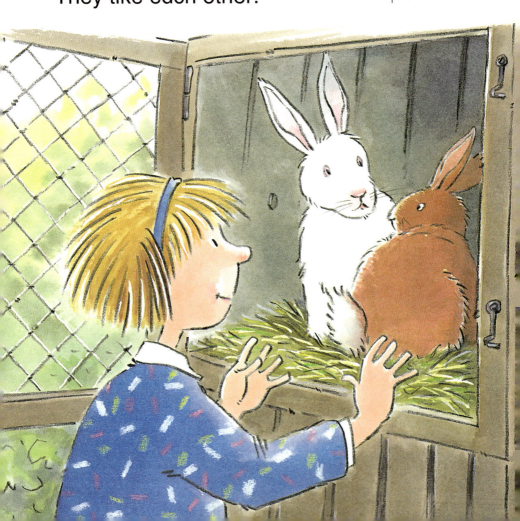

One day, Uta notices that Snow White has a fat tummy.

Uta's mother says: "Aha. Snow White will have babies soon," she says. "Lots and lots of baby rabbits. And Bommel is the father."

"Lots of baby rabbits? Well, then I can give the babies away as presents," Uta says.

"Yes, that is a good idea," her mother says. "But I hope somebody wants them!"

Uta hopes so, too.

bemerkt
Schneewittchen;
Bauch

wird ... haben

die Jungen
verschenken

The big day arrives. They all stand round the rabbit hutch. The children do not want to disturb Snow White, so they are very quiet. Then Snow White starts to push – and soon the first little baby comes out. The baby is small and a bit slimy.

"Ugh!" Uta says. She wipes the baby with straw. Soon it is clean.

Kaninchenstall

stören; Schneewittchen

pressen

schmierig

reibt ab

Then she puts the baby rabbit very close to Snow White.

Schneewittchen

Snow White has five babies altogether! The children clean them all. Soon the babies look like little balls of wool.

kleine Wollknäuels

All except for one. It has a white head and white ears and a white tail like Snow White. But its fur is reddish-brown.

bis auf

Fell

19

Snow White looks very tired. She licks her babies. How sweet!

"We must give the babies something to drink!" Uta says.

Schneewittchen; müde

leckt ab

"Don't worry," Uta's mother says. "They know what to do." Soon the babies start to drink their mother's milk.

And when all the babies are full, they sleep beside their mother. Sweet little babies!

Uta looks up and says: "I think the babies need a sunshade. It's very sunny here."

"Good idea," her mother says.

Uta goes to the garage and gets a big sunshade and puts it up. Then she gets some water for Snow White, and some food. But Snow White is not hungry at the moment.

satt

Sonnenschirm

Schneewittchen

She is too tired. She lies there in the straw, with all her little babies around her like little balls of wool. Sweet little babies!

And Bommel? He is in the hutch next door. He is asleep!

"Wake up, Bommel!" Uta says. "You've got five children!"

	müde
	kleine Wollknäuels
	Käfig

sunshade

The chocolate bunny hunt

Willy is a hunting dog. He belongs to our neighbour. Willy likes to hunt everything. He hunts slippers, carpets, cakes, biscuits, apples and bananas. Everything he sees! He bites the big things, and swallows the little ones!

"That dog must be trained," Mummy says sometimes, when Willy hunts things. But training him is the job of our neighbour.

Jagdhund

gehört

jagen
Hausschuhe;
Teppiche

verschluckt
muss erzogen werden

On Easter Sunday we always go for a morning walk with Daddy. Mummy hides Easter eggs and chocolate bunnies in the garden. We are very excited and happy.

When we come back from our morning walk, we go to the garden. Then we start to look for the eggs and the chocolate bunnies.

versteckt; Ostereier; Schokoladenhasen

And there, right in the middle of the tulips, is the first chocolate bunny. Suddenly, Willy runs over and picks up the rabbit himself! We rub our eyes, and then we start to laugh. Willy has the Easter bunny in his mouth. He wags his tail.
   We laugh and laugh, but Mummy is angry. "Why can't our neighbour keep the dog in his garden?" Mummy is sad because Easter Sunday is different from the way she wanted.

genau in der Mitte; Tulpen

Schokoladen-hase

Plötzlich

reiben

wedelt mit dem Schwanz

anders, als sie erwartet hatte

One hour later, Mummy is happy again. We have found all the bunnies and eggs, and now we are sitting on the terrace and are eating cake.

haben gefunden

Terrasse

Then Willy runs over to us again.
"What has he done this time?" Mummy wonders.
Willy digs a hole in the garden. Then he takes something out of the hole.

Was hat er jetzt schon wieder angestellt?; fragt sich

gräbt; Loch

He comes over to us with a dirty old bone in his mouth. He puts it on Mummy's lap. "Oh no!" she says. We start to laugh.

"You see?" Daddy says. "He feels sorry. That's a present because of the bunny. He really is well-trained after all!"

Knochen

Schoß

Es tut ihm Leid

gut erzogen

bone

The walk

Anne has a canary. His name is Pumpernickel. He has blue feathers and his throat is black and white. He sits on the perch in his cage and chirps all day long.

    Pumpernickel is a happy canary. Anne gives him new seed and fresh water every day. At night she puts a blanket over his cage, because canaries like to sleep in the dark, and don't like draughts.

Kanarienvogel

Hals

Stange

zwitschert

Samen

(Woll)Decke

Zugluft

The doorbell rings. Anne opens the door. It's Klara. Klara's pram is outside the house, and inside the pram is Klara's rabbit Bert. Bert looks funny because he is tucked up in a blanket.

Kinderwagen

ist eingewickelt

pram

"I want to go for a walk with Bert. Do you want to come with me?" Klara asks.

"Oh yes," Anne answers. She turns round. But who can *she* take on the walk? She can't take Daddy's goldfish. They only swim in the aquarium.

29

Suddenly Anna has an idea.
She goes to her room and
gets her old dolly's pram.
She takes out all the
cushions, and pushes it to
Pumpernickel's cage. She
picks up the cage and puts it
in the pram. Then she goes to
Klara and says:
"Pumpernickel needs
some fresh air,
too. Let's go!"

Plötzlich

Puppenwagen

Kissen

Pumpernickel is on his perch. He looks around. He is very happy. Anna brings the blanket along, too, just in case – because canaries don't like draughts.

Then they walk towards the playground. People stop and stare. Anna and Klara laugh each time. Animals are more interesting than dollies!

The playground is windy. Anne takes the blanket and puts it over the cage. Then she says to Pumpernickel:

"You must sit in the dark now. But I can still tell you what happens in the playground."

Stange

(Woll)Decke

Zugluft

Spielplatz

starren

Puppen

Then Anne describes the swing, the slide and the maze. Pumpernickel chirps under his blanket. Klara scratches her rabbit behind the ears so that he doesn't get bored.

	beschreibt Schaukel; Rutschbahn Labyrinth; zwitschert
	(Woll)Decke
	kratzt
	ihm nicht langweilig wird

"Perhaps we can give Bert some fresh grass?" Klara says.

"Good idea! There's some grass beside the maze," Anne answers.

Klara takes Bert out of the pram and puts him in the grass. He sniffs and hops.

Kinderwagen

Klara leans over to get him some grass – and then it happens!

beugt sich vor

Bert hops away! Right into the **maze**! Klara and Anne run after him. They go deeper and deeper inside the maze.

Finally Klara says: "I've got him! But how can we find our way out of here again?"

Labyrinth

Schließlich

Anne and Klara cannot remember the way out!
Suddenly they hear an angry chirping noise. "It's Pumpernickel!" Anne says. "He's bored under the blanket." Anne and Klara run towards the chirping sound. "Pumpernickel showed us the way out of the maze!" Anne says happily. "It's very lucky we brought him along!"

remember	sich erinnern
Suddenly	Plötzlich
chirping noise	Zwitschergeräusch
He's bored	Ihm ist langweilig
blanket	(Woll)Decke
showed	zeigte
maze	Labyrinth
brought him along	ihn mitgebracht haben

Oscar the kitten

Oscar is my favourite kitten. His mother Rosa has four babies, and Oscar is very special. He is grey and white, and he has black dots on his back. I think Oscar looks like a fluffy little ball of wool! The other kittens are nice too, but I like Oscar the best. I think Oscar likes me, too. He always comes when I call him. I stroke him a lot, and I think he is the best kitten in the whole world.

Kätzchen

Punkte

flaumiger kleiner Wollknäuel

streichle

One day Daddy and Mummy go out, and my friend Eva comes to visit me. We let Oscar and the other kittens run around the house. And they wee-wee everywhere! We wash everything, and spray deodorant.

When Mummy and Daddy come home, Daddy says: "What's that funny smell?"

Kätzchen

voll pinkeln

sprühen
(Deo)Spray

Daddy sniffs the carpet and says: "My carpet stinks! You didn't let the kittens in here, did you?"

Eva and I are embarrassed. We have made a mistake. Daddy is angry. Very angry.

	riecht am Teppich
	stinkt
	ihr habt nicht … gelassen
	oder
	verlegen
	haben gemacht

Daddy and Mummy go to work the next day. I put a cat litter in the kitchen, and teach the kittens how to use it. Oscar is a bit stupid. He always wees beside the cat litter, instead of into it! We make sure he doesn't wee on Daddy's carpet again.

Katzenklo
Kätzchen; wie es zu gebrauchen ist

pinkelt

Just when we think Oscar is trained, he wees in the middle of the floor. What can I do? I am very sad.

erzogen; pinkelt; mitten auf

My birthday is next week. Daddy asks me what I want, and I say: "I want to keep Oscar."

möchte behalten

Daddy looks angry. I know what that means.

bedeutet

Before my birthday there is a Sunday. The kittens are outside playing.

Kätzchen

Then we hear a scratching noise at the door. The kittens want to come in. They start to miaow and to hiss.

Kratz-geräusch

fauchen

And the miaowing and hissing gets louder and louder.

They want to come into the house. Daddy is angry and says: "I don't want those kittens in here."

Kätzchen

Stupid Daddy.

Then Mummy gets up and opens the door for them.

The kittens march into the kitchen, go into the cat litter, do a wee-wee inside it, and then go back outside to their basket.

marschieren

Katzenklo

pinkeln

Korb

We all stand there, very surprised.

überrascht

Daddy says: "Goodness me!"

(Ach) du meine Güte!

Mummy says: "Where did they learn to do that?" Then she says: "Well, if they know how to do that ..." and she looks at Daddy.

lernten sie

Nun, wenn sie wissen, wie es geht ...

"Do you think we can keep Oscar?" I ask Daddy.

And then Daddy and Mummy nod their heads!

nicken mit dem Kopf

I give them a big hug and say: "Thank you! Oscar is the best birthday present in the world!"

Umarmung

The Dog in the Church

Max is Moritz's dog. He follows him wherever he goes. Except to school.

Moritz is in the choir now. They sing in the church on Sunday. Max is not allowed to go there, either.

Today is Moritz's first church service. He wakes up early, and is very nervous. He does not go for a walk with Max. Max is nervous too, because he wants to go out with Moritz.

wohin (auch immer)

Außer

Kirchenchor

darf auch nicht

Gottesdienst

Finally Moritz goes to church. He stands with the other children at the altar. They pray and then they sing.
　Suddenly people start to talk. A dog walks down the aisle.

Endlich

beten

Plötzlich

Gang

Everyone looks. The dog goes up to the front and sits down next to Moritz. He sits up straight, just like a choirboy.

setzt sich aufrecht hin; genau wie

Chorjunge

Moritz doesn't know what to do. He is very embarrassed. His heart beats hard.

Then the sexton comes and pulls at Max's lead. He is angry. He pulls Max out of the church.

Then the choir starts to sing a hymn.

Then people hear the dog come into the church again! Max goes down the aisle, up to the front, sits beside Moritz – and then "sings" with the choir! What a terrible howling noise! The choir bravely finishes the hymn. Everybody laughs.

Moritz is very worried and embarrassed now. What will the priest say?

When the church service is over, the priest goes over to Moritz and Max.

verlegen

klopft

Küster

zieht; Hundeleine

Loblied

Gang

heulendes Geräusch; tapfer

beunruhigt

Gottesdienst

He laughs and says: "You have a nice dog there – but I think he needs some singing lessons, don't you?"

Gesangsstunden

Felix is back

Felix is not a child. Felix is a little hamster. Let me tell you how I found him.

I want to put on my roller skates. Suddenly I hear a strange noise. A funny squeaking, like someone calling for help. But it must be someone very small and weak.

I look down through the grating above the cellar. I can see something small and brown. How can I get to it? Suddenly I have an idea.

fand	
Plötzlich	
seltsames Geräusch	
Quieken	
..., der um Hilfe ruft	
Schwaches	
Gitter; Keller	

I can go to the cellar and try to reach the animal through the window. I run down the stairs, open the cellar window – and see the little brown animal. It looks like a hamster.

Keller

herankommen an

grating

I call upstairs: "Kai, come down, there's a hamster here." But Kai can't hear me. He is not interested anyway. He wants to play with his toy cars.

sowieso nicht interessiert

"Hey, Kai, there's a hamster downstairs!"

Kai looks up. "A hamster?" he asks.

I nod at him. "Yes, a hamster!"

nicke

Kai suddenly gets up, and says: "Where?" Kai wants to have a hamster or a guinea-pig of his own, but Mummy says he can't, because an animal means a lot of work.

plötzlich

sein eigenes Meerschweinchen

bedeutet

"Come on, Kai, I'll show you where it is," I say, and Kai and I walk down the cellar stairs together. I show Kai the tiny frightened animal. It looks at us with big eyes, and shivers.

ich werde dir zeigen

Kellertreppe

winzige

verängstigte

zittert

48

"I want him!" Kai says.
"What about me?" I ask.
"Well okay," Kai says. "We can share him. But we must call him Felix!"

uns teilen

I'm not sure I want to share him, but we have other problems at the moment. How can we convince Mummy that we can look after Felix?

Kai decides to clear his room. I find a shoe box to keep the trembling hamster in.

teilen

überzeugen

beschließt; aufzuräumen

aufbewahren; zitternden

Kai looks at the clock: "If we hurry we can make supper and give Mummy a nice surprise!"

We quickly get the kitchen ready. Kai lays the table and boils some eggs. Then we take sausage and cheese from the fridge.

Überraschung

deckt den Tisch

kocht

Wurst

Kühlschrank

We even put napkins and flowers on the table. And all because of little Felix the hamster!

Servietten

napkin

Exhausted, we sit in the kitchen and start to plan. First we must find out where the hamster comes from. We hope that we can keep him.

Erschöpft

behalten

Then Kai remembers that Felix needs something to eat, too. He runs outside, grabs some grass, and stuffs it in the shoe box. The shoe box looks like quite a cosy home for a hamster!

erinnert sich

packt

wirklich gemütliches Zuhause

"What do hamsters eat apart from grass?" I ask.

"Carrots, vegetables, lettuce, and seed, of course," Kai says. He takes a lettuce leaf and a carrot from the fridge and puts them in Felix's box.

| abgesehen von |
| Gemüse; Kopfsalat |
| Samen |
| Salatblatt |

He starts to eat right away. Kai gives the hamster a little bowl of water, too.

Just then, Mummy comes home. She looks tired.

She looks at us: "What have you got there?"

Kai gets up quickly and says: "Lisa found him. He belongs to us, because we really need a hamster."

| Schüssel |
| müde |
| fand; gehört |

Mummy stands there, puts her hands on her hips and says: "Now just a moment. Who does the hamster belong to?"

Hüften

gehört

"To us, of course!" Kai says. "And he likes to eat our carrots, too. He loves it here."

"Mummy," Kai says, "if Felix doesn't belong to anyone, can we have him? Please? We'll look after him. And we'll always tidy our rooms."

Mummy gives a sigh. She looks at the laid table and has a think. Then she asks: "Can you really look after him all by yourselves?"

"Yes, of course!" we say. I think Mummy likes the way we laid the table. Because now we're allowed to keep Felix!

Seufzer

gedeckten Tisch

(ganz) allein

wir ... behalten dürfen

The snake in the loo

Fabian goes up to his Mummy and says: "Florian, the boy next door, has got a snake."

Fabian is interested in his new neighbours. He wants a friend so that he can play. Then he sees Florian. Florian asks Fabian if he wants to see what he has got in his room. Fabian says "yes" and goes with him.

Schlange
interessiert sich für

Nachbarn

Fabian sees a large glass box in one corner of the room. It is called a terrarium. There is a big snake inside.

"It's not dangerous at all!" Florian says. "Most people think that snakes are dangerous, but they're not."

*Ecke
nennt sich;
Terrarium*

Schlange

terrarium

Fabian goes to his mother and says: "He really has got a snake. It's his pet!"

Schlange

His mother shakes her head: "How can anyone keep a snake? They're dangerous!"

halten

"This snake is different," Fabian says. "Florian says that snakes are not always dangerous. Some of them are, and some of them are not. And this one is not."

The next day the doorbell rings. It's Florian.

"My snake is gone," he says. "Disappeared."

ist weg

Verschwunden

Florian is very upset.

bestürzt

"The s-snake is gone? I d-don't believe it!" Fabian stammers.

glaube

stottert

His mother stands behind him. "There, you see? It's just like I told you!"

Siehst du?

sagte

58

Fabian is embarrassed about his mother. He bites his lips. But he knows that she is right.

Days go by, and everyone looks for the snake. They look under tables and behind cupboards and under beds and under the loo and behind the bathroom cupboard and beside the bath and in the shower and inside the towels. Nobody can find the snake. They look in Fabian's house and in Florian's house. It's no good. The snake is gone.

verlegen	
beißt sich auf	
Tage vergehen	
Schlange	
Klo	
Handtücher	
Es hilft nichts	
ist weg	

loo

Fabian sits on the loo. He wonders where the snake is. He gets up, and pulls up his trousers.

Suddenly he sees something green beside the toilet seat. Fabian shouts, slams the bathroom door and calls out loudly: "The snake! The snake!" Then he runs over to Florian's house and rings the bell.

Schlange

Plötzlich

schlägt ... zu

"Where is it?" Florian asks.
"Beside our loo! Behind the cupboard, I think!" Fabian says. There is a hot-water pipe there. It is dark and warm – and that's what snakes like.

	Klo
	Heißwasser-leitung
	Schlangen

Florian grabs the snake and takes it over to his terrarium. There are leaves and earth inside it. The snake curls up in the leaves and looks happy again.

	packt
	Terrarium
	Blätter; Erde
	rollt sich zusammen

"It's beautiful, isn't it?" Florian whispers. The snake's skin is a greenish-gold colour.

	oder
	flüstert
	Haut; grün-goldene Farbe

"Yes," Fabian says.

And then they watch the lovely shiny snake slowly curl up into the leaves inside the terrarium.

It's hard to believe that such a harmless snake can cause so much of a fuss!

	schwer; glauben
	harmlose
	Wirbel

Dein Wörterbuch   A–P

A	anyway	sowieso, irgendwie, ohnehin, trotzdem
	apart from	abgesehen von
B	bowl	Schüssel
	brave	tapfer, mutig, unerschrocken
C	carpet	Teppich
	cellar	Keller
	corner	Ecke
	cushion	Kissen
D	dot	Punkt
E	earth	Erde
	except for	bis auf
F	finally	endlich, schließlich, endgültig

F	for a while	eine Zeit lang
	fridge	Kühlschrank
H	hard	schwer, fest, kräftig, anstrengend
I	important	wichtig
	in the middle of	mitten in, auf
J	just like	genau wie
L	lettuce	Kopfsalat
N	napkin	Serviette
	neighbour	Nachbar
P	playground	Spielplatz
	pram	Kinderwagen

Dein Wörterbuch S–T

S
sausage	Wurst
skin	Haut
slide	Rutschbahn
slippers	Hausschuhe
sunshade	Sonnenschirm
surprise	Überraschung
swing	Schaukel

T
throat	Hals, Kehle, Rachen
to be embarrassed	verlegen sein
to be exhausted	erschöpft sein
to be frightened	Angst haben
to be surprised	überrascht sein
to be tired	müde sein
to be upset	bestürzt, mitgenommen, ärgerlich sein
to be worried	besorgt, beunruhigt sein

T	to beat	klopfen, schlagen
	to believe	glauben, denken, meinen
	to boil	kochen
	to clear	aufräumen
	to convince	überzeugen
	to cool	kühlen, abkühlen (lassen)
	to decide	sich entscheiden, sich entschließen
	to describe	beschreiben, schildern, darstellen
	to dig	(aus-, um)graben, ausheben
	to disappear	verschwinden
	to disturb	stören, unterbrechen
	to grab	packen, schnappen, an sich reißen
	to hide	verstecken, verbergen, verheimlichen
	to hurt	wehtun, verletzen, verwunden

Dein Wörterbuch   T–W

T

to keep	aufbewahren, (be)halten, einhalten, (be)hüten
to lay the table	den Tisch decken
to lean over	sich vorbeugen, sich neigen
to mean	bedeuten, meinen, denken, beabsichtigen
to nod	nicken
to notice	bemerken, wahrnehmen, zur Kenntnis nehmen
to pull	ziehen, zerren, reißen
to push	stoßen, drücken, schieben
to reach	(her)ankommen an, (er)reichen, gehen bis zu
to remember	sich erinnern an, denken an
to rub	abreiben, einreiben, polieren
to scratch	kratzen
to share	(sich) teilen
to slam	zuschlagen